HAL•LEONARD
INSTRUMENTAL
PLAY-ALONG

AUDIO
ACCESS
INCLUDED

ALTO SAX

BEST OF
METALLICA

T0210279

PLAYBACK+
Speed • Pitch • Balance • Loop

To access audio, visit:
www.halleonard.com/mylibrary

Enter Code
5578-3042-1984-2460

Recorded by Scott Seelig

Cherry Lane Music Company
Educational Director/Project Supervisor: Susan Poliniak
Director of Publications: Mark Phillips
Publications Coordinator: Rebecca Skidmore

ISBN: 978-1-60378-119-0

HAL•LEONARD®

Visit Hal Leonard Online at
www.halleonard.com

Contact us:
Hal Leonard
7777 West Bluemound Road
Milwaukee, WI 53213
Email: info@halleonard.com

In Europe, contact:
Hal Leonard Europe Limited
42 Wigmore Street
Marylebone, London, W1U 2RN
Email: info@halleonardeurope.com

In Australia, contact:
Hal Leonard Australia Pty. Ltd.
4 Lentara Court
Cheltenham, Victoria, 3192 Australia
Email: info@halleonard.com.au

CONTENTS

The Day That Never Comes

Music by Metallica
Lyrics by James Hetfield

ALTO SAX

Enter Sandman

Words and Music by
James Hetfield, Lars Ulrich and Kirk Hammett

ALTO SAX

Fade to Black

Words and Music by
James Hetfield, Lars Ulrich,
Cliff Burton and Kirk Hammett

ALTO SAX

Harvester of Sorrow

Words and Music by
James Hetfield and Lars Ulrich

ALTO SAX

Nothing Else Matters

Words and Music by
James Hetfield and Lars Ulrich

ALTO SAX

One

Words and Music by
James Hetfield and Lars Ulrich

ALTO SAX

Sad but True

Words and Music by
James Hetfield and Lars Ulrich

ALTO SAX

Seek & Destroy

Words and Music by
James Hetfield and Lars Ulrich

ALTO SAX **Moderate Rock**

The Thing That Should Not Be

Words and Music by
James Hetfield, Lars Ulrich and Kirk Hammett

ALTO SAX

The Unforgiven

Words and Music by
James Hetfield, Lars Ulrich and Kirk Hammett

ALTO SAX

Until It Sleeps

Words and Music by
James Hetfield and Lars Ulrich

ALTO SAX

Moderate Rock

Welcome Home (Sanitarium)

Words and Music by
James Hetfield, Lars Ulrich and Kirk Hammett

ALTO SAX

14